Introduction

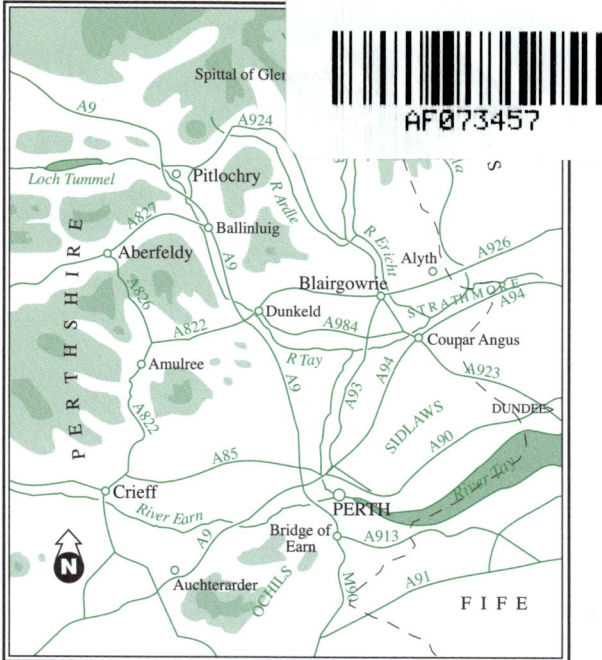

As the roadside notices proclaim to visitors entering Perthshire, this is 'the Heart of Scotland', which is both a geographical statement and a bold assertion that here is the essence of all that is to be found elsewhere in Scotland.

This is not altogether true: the west coast, the Atlantic islands, the Borders abbeys and the Solway find no mirror in Perthshire, but so much else does. Hills and heather are in abundant supply, as are rivers and lochs; the county is big enough to contain both the well-known examples – Ben Lawers and Schiehallion, Loch Tummel and Loch Rannoch – and also scores of lesser humps and lesser waters, known only to the shepherds or to the more imaginative walkers.

Perthshire is more, of course, than just topography; here are the ancient capitals of Scone and Forteviot, here are the battle-sites of Killiecrankie and – perhaps – Mons Graupius. There are certainly Roman remains and there are innumerable links with the Stewart dynasty and its vicissitudes, right through to the final down-turn in its fortunes in 1746.

Ossian's Hall (Walks 12 & 23)

The walks in this book – which covers the eastern end of the county – will also bring the visitor into contact with aspects of workaday Perthshire, past and present: the bleachfields and linen manufactories of Perth, Luncarty, Almondbank, and Blairgowrie; the reed-beds and the thatching industry of the Tay estuary; the coastal shipping trade operating out of Perth; and the famous berry-fields of Strathmore. Plus – in many shapes and guises – the quintessentially modern industry of tourism.

Then there is the built heritage: the 'folly' on Kinnoull Hill, Scone Palace, Dunkeld Cathedral, Ossian's Hall on the Braan and Dalnaglar Castle in Glen Shee.

From the walker's point of view, Perthshire divides quite naturally into the Highland and the Lowland; divided by the Highland Line (a geological fault line). The walks described here lie on both sides of that natural division. There are some which rise only a few metres above sea level and offer no views of even distant mountains; and there are others which offer the key romantic elements which attracted the first tourists: pine woods, falling water, the purple of the heather and the prospect of the hills.

We suggest there is enough for everyone. Enjoy your walking.

Perth and the River Tay, viewed from the rail bridge (Walk 20)

1 The Cateran Trail _____ A/B/C

A waymarked, long-distance footpath on paths and public roads, passing through the gentle hill country of north-east Perthshire. Some of the routes in this guide follow parts of the Trail, which can be used to link them. For further information, visit www.pkct.org/cateran-trail.

O.S. Sheets 43, 44 & 53

In the northern part of the area covered by this book you will come across paths marked by posts bearing a red heart symbol. These paths are part of the Cateran Trail: a waymarked circuit of 64 miles/103km.

The trail – named after the highland cattle reivers who once followed these tracks when plundering the area – starts in Blairgowrie, runs north to Bridge of Cally, then makes a loop through Strathardle, Glen Shee and Glen Isla.

Blairgowrie sits on the edge of the fertile farmland of Strathmore. As the path leads northwards it enters hillier, moorland country, but there is only one significant climb: the hill-crossing between Enochdhu and Spittal of Glenshee (*see* Walk 2).

The route of the trail is complicated in places, following a variety of rough footpaths, tracks, forest roads and minor public roads. It is possible to walk the whole trail, using settlements along the way for overnight accommodation, but most walkers walk the Trail in sections. Two of the best sections are described in this guide: Blairgowrie to Bridge of Cally (Walk 8) and Enochdhu to Spittal of Glenshee (Walk 2). Other routes use parts of the trail (Walks 4, 5 and 6).

In addition, Walk 3 is waymarked as part of the Trail and can be used to create a loop of 20 miles/32km when combined with Walk 2 and the path down the east side of Glen Shee (*see* map).

2 Enochdhu to Spittal of Glenshee A

A moderate hill walk, on good tracks or paths for most of the way, linking two small settlements. **Length: 6 miles/10km** (one way); **Height Climbed: 1300ft/400m**.

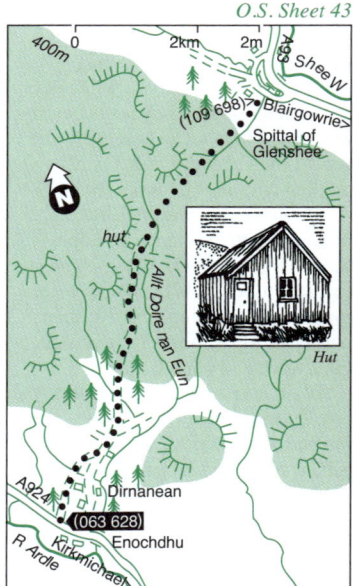

O.S. Sheet 43

The start of this route, marked by signs for the right of way and the Cateran Trail, lies at the western edge of the little cluster of houses at Enochdhu in Strathardle.

The first part of the route is a good rough track leading up to a group of estate buildings. Pass through these and continue. You reach a signposted junction in an open area with conifers to your left. The main track keeps straight on, through open ground, but you go left, passing through a metal gate in a deer fence. Follow the track through the trees to reach a similar gate at the top of the plantation. You are now on the open moor.

Follow the track up the left-hand side of a shallow, heathery glen. Approaching the watershed, a track goes right to cross the burn (ignore), just beyond which you pass a tin-roofed hut and continue climbing.

At the watershed there is a gate. The view ahead opens out quite suddenly and the major peaks of Glen Shee come into sight: The Cairnwell (3059ft) commanding the pass at the head of the glen and, closer to hand, Ben Gulabin (2641ft).

This spot is the dividing line between the softer contours of Strathardle and the more mountainous country of Glen Shee. Below the new horizon of peaks nestles the objective of the day, the settlement at Spittal of Glenshee. The old coaching inn burned down in 1957, and the hotel which replaced it in 2014.

From the watershed, there remains only an easy descent over grassy slopes by a burn, before reaching the road at another right of way sign.

It is difficult to link the two ends of the walk using public transport, so either arrange to be picked up or return by the same route.

3 Kirkmichael to Lair _____ A

A low hill-crossing of moderate length. Length: **5 miles/8km** *(one way); Height Climbed:* **800ft/250m**. *NB: Route pathless at either end – navigation skills required. Grazing animals on route.*

O.S. Sheet 43

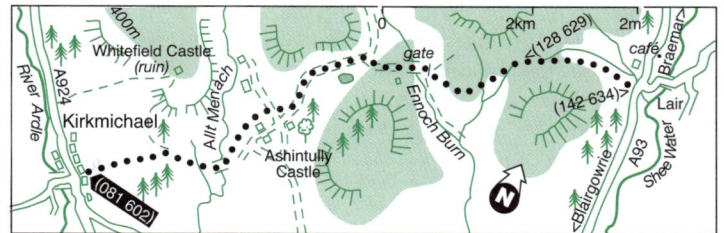

Start this walk from Kirkmichael: a small village in Strathardle, midway between Pitlochry and Blairgowrie on the A924. A few steps east of the bridge over the River Ardle, in the centre of the village, a right of way sign marks the start of this route.

The walk starts along a sunken track, but shortly gives way first to fields then to open moor. A faint path heads straight up the slope towards the northern (left-hand) tip of a belt of conifer woodland visible ahead.

At the end of the woodland, an arrow on a post points to a metal gate. Go through this. Looking ahead you see a further pedestrian gate to the left of a field gate. Head for this. Once through that gate, further posts lead to a footbridge over Allt Menach.

Go through a gate beyond the bridge then walk across a field to a further gate. (These gates and posts mark the detour past Ashintully Castle.) Keep to the right-hand side of the next two fields, with the wall of the castle grounds to your right, and you eventually arrive at a gate leading on to a broad track.

Cross the track and continue (Lair) to reach a track heading north from the castle. Go left on the track. Continue, passing a small loch, to reach a junction. Go right on a rough track (arrow).

Drop to cross the Ennoch Burn on a footbridge, then follow a faint path beyond, through a gate. At this point, some care is needed with navigation. Avoid the path heading down the burn to your right and look ahead-right to identify a marker post on the horizon. Follow a grassy path which edges up and across the slope to reach the post then continues to the watershed.

From here, the path is often unclear but the route (marked by helpful posts) continues, through heather and marsh, eventually reaching the A93 at the Lair, where there is a further right of way sign to mark the start at this end.

4 River Ericht / 5 The Knockie ——————— C/C

4) *A short walk up the wooded den of the Ericht on the northern edge of Blairgowrie, passing the Falls of Ericht and the town's old jute mills. Length:* **2 miles/3km**; *Height Climbed:* negligible. **5)** *An easy hill climb on the outskirts of Blairgowrie, providing fine views over Strathmore and of the edge of the Highlands. The walk follows metalled roads and clear, rough tracks. Length:* **3 miles/5km**; *Height Climbed:* **500ft/150m**. *The two walks can be combined to create a walk with a total length of* **3½ miles/5.5km** *(see map).* **NB:** *both walks follow sections of the Cateran Trail (see Walk 1).*

O.S. Sheet 53

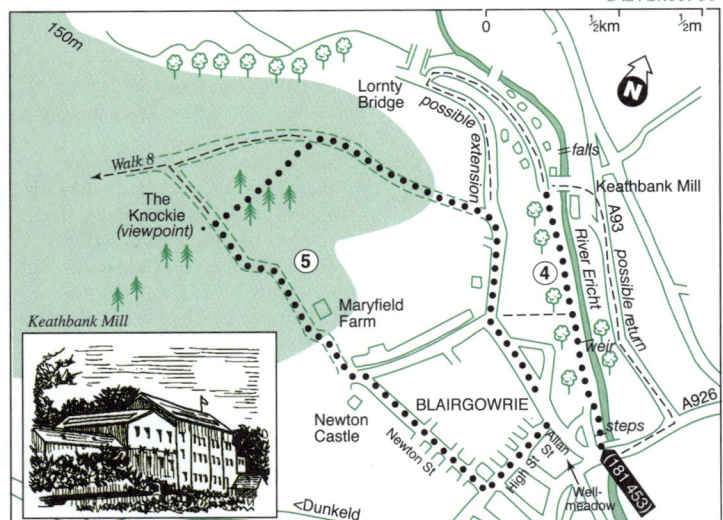

Blairgowrie, now a busy service centre and dormitory town for Perth, was once noted for its jute production, with the swift waters of the River Ericht being used to power a number of mills. These ruined or refurbished buildings are still visible today.

Walk 4) For ease, convenience and variety, the riverside walk from the centre of Blairgowrie is to be recommended. Start on the road bridge over the River Ericht, noting the view upstream of the weir, the lade and the jute mills which once used the water from the river.

Having enjoyed the view, return

to the Blairgowrie (west) end of the bridge and turn right down a flight of steps to reach the start of the riverside path. At first there is an open, grassy area to your left. Just after this park ends the valley narrows and you climb a flight of steps to your left to join a track.

Turn right along this track and continue up the wooded valley, passing the Falls of Ericht – a narrowing of the river incorporating Cargill's Leap, where a fleeing 17th-century Covenanter had to jump for his life. You reach a footbridge over the Ericht, with the impressive bulk of the old Keathbank Mill (a reminder of the former textile activity in the town) on the far side of the river. At this point you have a choice.

The easiest return is simply to retrace your steps. If you wish to extend your walk, continue up the river, passing further ruined and converted mill buildings, until you join a narrow public road. Turn left down the road to return to the start through farmland. If you wish to extend your walk even further, watch for the junction with a track signposted for the Knockie Path heading off to your right (*see* map). Turn on to this and follow the reverse of Walk 5 to return to the start.

Walk 5) From the centre of Blairgowrie, walk out of the Wellmeadow up Allan Street (signposted as the path to Bridge of Cally), quickly swinging left into High Street. Continue along this road until Newton Street starts to the right.

Turn onto this and follow it uphill to a T-junction. To the left here is Newton Castle, the 17th-century home of the Chief of the Clan Macpherson.

Turn left at the junction and follow a track which swings right, passing Maryfield Farm, and climbs up to the low summit of The Knockie. There is a bench here and a viewfinder which names the main features of the view.

If you wish to link with Walk 8, carry straight on beyond, dropping down the far side of the hill on a path between fields. When this joins a farm track turn left. **If you wish to return to Blairgowrie**, turn right from the viewpoint on a rough path through woodland on the ridge of the hill. Join a field edge by a bench and continue a short way to join a metalled road. Turn right down this to reach a junction with a public road.

For the quickest return from this point, turn right along the public road. If you wish to extend the route, turn left along the public road then right at the junction shortly before Lornty Bridge to follow the reverse of Walk 4 back to Blairgowrie.

Former mill by the River Ericht

6 Hill of Alyth & Hill of Loyal / 7 Den o' Alyth_B/C

6) *A rewarding 'holiday walk' for the non mountain-goer, with superb views encompassing Strathmore, the Sidlaws and the mountains flanking upper Glen Isla. Length:* **3 miles/5km**; *Height Climbed:* **760ft/230m**.
7) *A network of paths in a wooded den. Length:* **2½ miles/4km** (there and back); *Height Climbed:* negligible.

O.S. Sheet 53

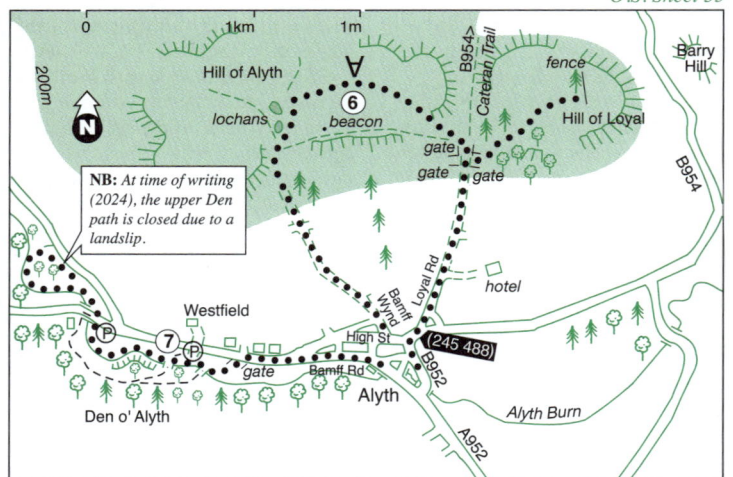

NB: *At time of writing (2024), the upper Den path is closed due to a landslip.*

Walk 6) This walk lies in the extreme east of Perthshire, the Angus boundary lying just east of these two hills. The hills are best done as a circuit, and the following description takes the walker to Hill of Loyal first, then to Hill of Alyth.

Park in the centre of Alyth and walk up the main road north (B952), by the east side of the Alyth Burn. At the top of the hill turn right (along Hill St) then first left up Loyal Road to start the path up Hill of Loyal.

The road runs past the entrance to Lands of Loyal Hotel and continues uphill. When the tarmac ends continue on a clear track. Ignore a track heading right and keep straight on. The gradient is steep at first, easing after ½ mile/0.8km. As it eases, one is faced by three gates.

The left-hand gate leads into a field; the middle one to Hill of Alyth (and the B954, along the line of the Cateran Trail – *see* Walk 1); and the right-hand one to Hill of Loyal.

If you wish to climb Hill of Loyal, go through the right-hand gate and cross a small stream to enter an area of open woodland. Follow a faint, rough track which climbs through the trees and gorse.

The sparse oak and larch woodland gives way shortly to open heather moor, and wide vistas open out, with Glen Isla and the bulk of the Grampians to the north and the wide expanse of Strathmore to the south, backed by the Sidlaws. The summit is unmarked but it is worth continuing east to a stand of larch by a fence, from where one obtains a superb view of Barry Hill – associated in legend with Queen Guinevere, wife of King Arthur – and its concentric rings of ancient vitrified fortifications. Return to the three gates by the same route.

If you wish to climb Hill of Alyth, take the middle gate. A yellow arrow points half-right, along the line of the Cateran Trail, but for this walk go half-left, climbing the slope on a grassy path through gorse. This leads eventually to more open ground, after which one simply heads upwards, the summit lying 700-800m from the gates. There is a direction indicator beside the trig point and an iron bench a few steps away, giving views over the village and on towards the Sidlaws.

To complete the circuit, continue another 500m or so westwards from the summit (ie, along the hummocky ridge). You should reach one of a pair of small lochans. Cross a dried stream bed below the more southerly (left-hand) lochan and continue downhill, aiming somewhat to the right, to pick up a fence-line running down towards an isolated stand of pines. From here you drop to join a clear track. Follow this as it drops down through young trees and fields towards the village, now clearly in view. When you reach the public road (Bamff Wynd) go left, then right to reach the High Street. Retrace your outward route from here to the centre of the village.

Walk 7) While you are in Alyth, it is worth visiting the Den o' Alyth: the wooded valley of the Alyth Burn to the west of the village.

This can be walked either from the main car park for the Den or from the centre of the village. If you are doing the latter, walk out of the west side of Market Square along Bamff Road. Follow this across the burn and beyond the edge of the village, then look for the entrance to the den to the left of the road. There are clear paths running by the burnside beyond.

1 *Balduff Hill* **2** *Badandun Hill* (740m) **3** *Craiglea Hill* **4** *Mayar* (928m) **5** *Dreish* (947m) **6** *Knock of Formal* **7** *Boustie Ley* (876m) **8** *Ben Tirran* (896m) **9** *Cat Law* (668m)

8 Blairgowrie to Bridge of Cally_____A

A pleasant walk over gentle moorland. Food and drink available at Bridge of Cally. Bus routes link Bridge of Cally to Blairgowrie. Length: **7 miles/11km** *(one way); Height Climbed: undulating,* **850ft/ 250m** *in total.* **NB:** *Can be wet in places; some navigation needed. Follows a section of the Cateran Trail (see Walk 1).*

O.S. Sheet 53

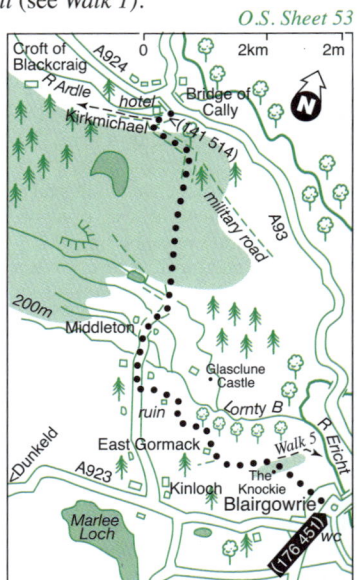

Start this route as for Walk 5 and continue to the junction with the metalled track beyond The Knockie. Turn left here (**NB:** from this point the route is signposted as part of the Cateran Trail – *see* Walk 1).

Turn right off the track just before the buildings at East Gormack and follow a well signposted route (Cateran Trail) along field edges for a mile/1.6km to join a minor public road. Turn right along this, crossing the Lornty Burn then climbing to the road's conclusion at the farm at Middleton.

Go straight through Middleton (leaving the farmhouse to your right) and continue beyond along a clear track which swings to the right, climbing gently.

After a little way there is a metal pedestrian gate to the left of the track, marked as part of the Cateran Trail. Go through this gate and follow a clear path between fences to reach a second gate. Go through this and rejoin the original track. Go left on this, passing through a pedestrian gate in a deer fence.

You are now on the open hill. After a short distance a signposted path heads left (Kirkmichael). Ignore this and continue, following a rough track with a dyke to your right.

The track can be wet in places as it runs across the open moorland, but the route is quite clear, eventually dropping down through the trees to reach a forest junction just short of Bridge of Cally. A turn to the left here will eventually lead to Kirkmichael along the Cateran Trail (8 miles/13km). To complete the current walk, however, turn right.

9 Atholl Woods Path   B

A signposted walk on good paths and tracks, through mixed woodland and over the open hill, with a possible extension to Loch Ordie. Length: **6¾ miles/11km**; *Height Climbed:* **500ft/150m**.

O.S. Sheet 52 or 53

To reach the Cally car park drive north from the centre of Dunkeld on the A923 Blairgowrie road. The road cuts sharp right at a junction just beyond the edge of the village. A short distance beyond this there is a signposted entrance to the car park on the left. Turn on to this track and follow it uphill through trees to a four-way junction. Turn left, into the car park.

Walk back to the junction and go left (Mill Dam) on a clear track. Follow this as it climbs gently, for 2 miles/3km, passing the Glen Glack cabins, by Cally Loch, then the houses at Upper Hatton and Birkenburn. At any junctions, follow the yellow markers.

Just before Mill Dam you reach a signposted junction. Keep straight on here (Loch Ordie), up the left-hand side of the lochan. Just beyond the end of the lochan there is a further junction. Go left here (Atholl Woods). (**NB:** If you keep straight on at this point it is a pleasant walk of 3 miles/5km to Loch Ordie.)

The clear track continues across open country for ½ mile/0.8km, then through forestry (all junctions are marked), before descending to reach a T-junction, with views over the Tay Valley opening up below. Go left at the junction and follow the track back into trees and down to the road.

Continue along the road as it bends round the crags and woods of Craig a Barns (the verge is narrow here; watch out for traffic). Just beyond little Polney Loch, to the left of the road, turn left and follow a clear track back to the car park.

10 Fiddler's Path / 11 Loch of the Lowes Path _B/B

Two waymarked walks from the centre of Dunkeld. **10)** *A circuit on riverside paths, plus a short section on the public road. Length:* **5½ miles/9km**; *Height Climbed:* **negligible**. **11)** *A circuit through woodlands, including a visit to a wildlife reserve. Length:* **4¾ miles/ 7.5km**; *Height Climbed:* **350ft/100m**. *For connected walks, see Walks 9, 13 and 14.*

O.S. Sheet 52 or 53

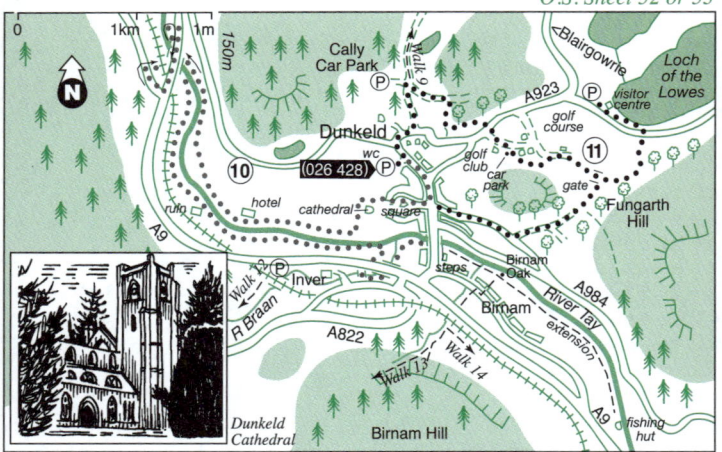

For both routes, park in the car park at the north end of the historic town of Dunkeld.

Walk 10) (*pale green markers*): Walk out of the car park and turn right, into the village. Turn right along High St, which quickly broadens out. Keep to the right (to visit the Cathedral, keep left, along Cathedral St). In the far right-hand corner of the square go through an arch marked 'Stanley Hill'. Keep left beyond this on a clear path, quickly reaching a junction with a second path. Go left along this.

The path runs along the fence around the cathedral. When the fence ends the path turns left and reaches a signposted junction. Keep straight on (Fiddler's Path) to join the clear path by the River Tay.

The path now runs clear for a little over 2 miles/3km. Follow the green markers at any junction, passing the Dunkeld House Hotel and continuing until the A9 crosses the river.

Follow the path under the bridge. Shortly beyond there is a signposted junction and a path leads right, up to the road. Turn right along the pavement. The road can be busy and the traffic fast, but you follow it for only a short distance. Having crossed the river, turn right down a side road.

In a short distance there is a signposted junction. For this walk go right (Fiddler's Path). The path passes beneath the railway line and the A9 then runs by the river.

As you approach Dunkeld the path turns right, up the River Braan. Pass under the A9, cross a footbridge and walk back down the other side of the Braan (ignoring a sign for Fiddler's Path pointing right). Follow the riverside path under the old stone road bridge. It is possible to continue by the river for a further 1½ miles/ 2.5km, but for this walk climb the steps by the bridge and cross the river to return to Dunkeld.

Walk 11 (*dark blue markers*): Walk out of the car park and turn left, by the main road. As this bends left, turn right up the A923 road for Blairgowrie. Follow this uphill, past an industrial estate, and take the next turn on the left (Cally Car Park). The track leads uphill to a crossroads. The car park is to the left, but for this walk go right (Loch of the Lowes) on a clear track through larch woodland.

Follow this track for around 500m until, as it climbs and begins to turn to left, an arrow indicates the start of a rough track to the right. Turn on to this then, after around ten paces, go right again (arrow), onto a broad path.

The path descends. As the public road comes into view watch for an arrow directing you up a small path to the left. Follow this above the road, through open beech wood. The path eventually drops to cross the public road just past the entrance to the Golf Club. Once over the road turn right, across a wooden walkway, then left, up the access road to the Club.

The road crosses the golf course – take care! When you reach the car park, ignore a right of way sign at the far left corner of the car park and look for the sign for Loch of the Lowes at the far right corner. The narrow path beyond leads down to a golf practice area. Keep to the left, go through a kissing gate, then on through fields at the foot of a slope, with houses up to your left.

At the end of the fields a further gate leads on to a rough track. Keep straight on, past a house and continue, climbing up on to Fungarth Hill.

When you pass though a wooden gate you have a choice:

To visit Loch of the Lowes Nature Reserve keep straight on, descending to join a narrow public road. Cross this and turn left for 250m to reach the Scottish Wildlife Trust visitor centre. The loch is known for ospreys in the summer and wildfowl in the winter. The centre is seasonal, but there is a hide which is open all year. Return the way you came to the junction.

To continue with the circuit turn right (signposted for Dunkeld) and follow the path as it merges with a broader track. This climbs to a gate then descends to join a clear track. Follow this down to a junction with the public road. Follow this road downhill to return to the start.

12 Braan Path & The Hermitage — B

A splendid signposted walk up a glen with fine woodland and 18th-century follies. Length: **4½ miles/7km**; Height Climbed: **250ft/80m**. *Possible links with Walks 13 and 23.*

O.S. Sheet 52 or 53

Park in the Hermitage car park (signposted off the A9, a mile west of the main Dunkeld turn-off). There are alternative car parks at Inver and Rumbling Bridge (*see map*).

Start along the clear track from the route map in the lower car park. A short way up the wooded glen there is a signposted split. Keep left here (this route is marked by a mixture of dark green markers and signs for 'Braan Path'). Continue, with the dramatic Falls of Braan to your left; passing Ossian's Hall, with its fine view of the falls, and Ossian's Cave along the way (two follies built for the 2nd Duke of Atholl in 1758).

Beyond the 'cave' the track pulls away from the river and leaves the cover of the trees; crossing an open area to join a quiet public road. Turn left along this, crossing Rumbling Bridge (above a waterfall). There is a lay-by just beyond. Beyond this, turn left on a path marked by a post. This leads up through woodland to the A822. Cross this (carefully) and continue up the clear track opposite.

Continue through open grazing land until you reach a signposted junction. Turn left here, following a clear track past Tomgarrow and on to a stile leading into an area of woodland. There are junctions with other routes in the plantation beyond, so keep an eye on the waymarking.

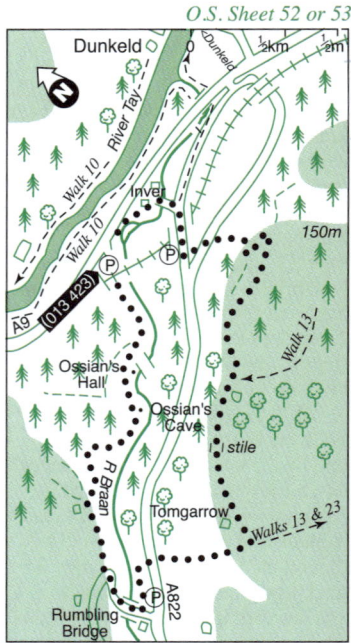

The paths lead you back down to the A822. Go straight across and follow a path downhill to join a minor road. Turn right along this, passing a car park to your left before crossing the railway then turning left, on a road bridge over the river, to reach the village of Inver.

Follow the road through Inver then continue on a path by the A9 for a short distance to return to the start.

13 Inchewan Path _____ B

A varied walk up a wooded den and over open ground. Length:
5 miles/8km; *Height Climbed:* **520ft/160m**. *Possible links with Walks 12, 14 and 23.*

O.S. Sheet 52 or 53

Start this walk opposite the Birnam Hotel, in the centre of the village of Birnam (there is limited roadside parking). A sign for the Inchewan Path points up Birnam Glen. Follow this metalled road, with a burn to your right, under the road and then the railway. At this point, watch for a path marked by arrows staring to your left.

The path leads up to a junction of tracks by a house. Keep straight on. After a few paces there is a signposted fork. Keep to the right (brown arrow), descending to a hairpin bend in the metalled track. Keep straight on at the bend, through a pedestrian gate, and start walking up the wooded glen of the Inchewan Burn.

After 1/2 mile/0.8km you reach a signposted junction at the start of the circuit. The route can be walked in either direction, but to follow this description go right, crossing the burn on a footbridge.

The path quickly joins a track. Go left (arrow). After a few paces you reach a junction with another track. Go left again (Inchewan Path).

Keep straight on at the next two junctions (arrows). At the third, go left (Inchewan, Braan), now on a path which is rougher but still clear. Go through a gate in a fence and follow the path beyond, which leads you out of the trees and on along a clear track, past the house at Tomgarrow and down to a clear junction.

Go left here (Inchewan) and follow the clear track through farmland (ignoring a path heading right for Bankfoot – see Walk 23) until you are approaching the buildings at Balhomish. Just before the buildings you cross a small burn. Immediately beyond this there is a stile to your left. Cross this and walk across a field, with the burn to your left, to enter the trees again. An arrow points ahead-right along a clear track. This leads you back to the junction by the Inchewan Burn, from where you retrace your route to the start.

Walks Perth, Dunkeld & Blairgowrie

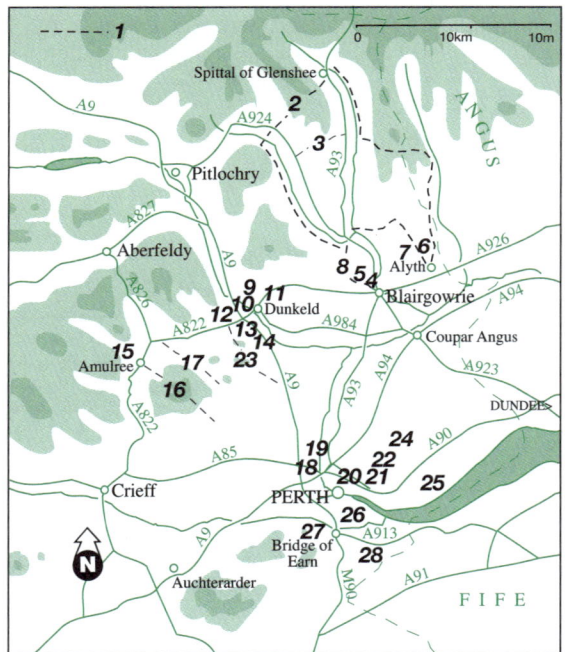

Grades

A ...... Full walking equipment required

B ...... Strong footwear and waterproof clothing required

C ...... Comfortable footwear recommended

Split Grades (eg: 'A/B') ..... A-grade if walked in its entirety;
B-grade if walked in part

— www.pocketwalks.com —

Published by: *Hallewell Publications, Scotland*
Printed in Scotland

While every care has been taken in the preparation of this guide, the publishers cannot accept responsibility for any loss, damage or injury resulting from its use.

Walks Perth, Dunkeld & Blairgowrie

walk	grade
1. The Cateran Trail	A/B/C
2. Enochdhu to Spittal of Glenshee	A
3. Kirkmichael to Lair	A
4. River Ericht	C
5. The Knockie	C
6. Hill of Alyth & Hill of Loyal	B
7. Den o' Alyth	C
8. Blairgowrie to Bridge of Cally	A
9. Atholl Woods Path	B
10. Fiddler's Path	B
11. Loch of the Lowes Path	B
12. Braan Path & The Hermitage	B
13. Inchewan Path	B
14. Birnam Hill Path	B
15. Loch Freuchie	B
16. Harrietfield to Amulree	A
17. Little Glenshee to Strath Braan	B
18. Perth to Almondbank	C
19. Perth to Luncarty	C
20. Perth to Kinnoull Tower	B
21. Kinnoull Hill	C
22. Deuchny Wood	C
23. Bankfoot to Rumbling Bridge	B
24. Dunsinane Hill	B/C
25. Errol & Port Allen	C
26. Moncreiffe Hill	B/C
27. Dunbarney & Silver Walks	C
28. Abernethy Glen	C

14 Birnam Hill Path _____ B

A signposted hill climb through mixed woodland, leading to fine views from an open summit. Length: **4¼ miles/7km**; *Height Climbed:* **1000ft/300m**. *Details of other walks in the area are provided on a map in the car park (see also Walks 9,10,11,12 & 13).*

O.S. Sheet 52 or 53

Birnam Hill, just to the south of Dunkeld/Birnam, offers fine views eastwards over Strathmore. On the horizon is the line of the Sidlaws, including the modest peak of Dunsinane Hill (*see* Walk 24): forever associated with Birnam Wood through Shakespeare's *Macbeth*.

To reach the start of the walk, drive south from Birnam on the A9 and turn first right onto the B867 for Bankfoot. After a short distance there is a car park to the right of the road.

This is one of the area's signposted walks, and the route is indicated by occasional red waymarkers. Pass under the railway line and, after a short distance, cut left on a signposted path. The climb is gentle at first, leading up to a fork in the path before Stair Bridge. A short detour on the left-hand path leads to the viewpoint; the main path goes right and climbs more steeply, over open ground, to the cairn on the wooded summit.

On the far side of the hill the descent is gentle at first, then steepens, down to join the track up the glen of the Inchewan Burn. If you go back-left at this point, up the glen, you are at the start of Walk 13. For this route, however, go right.

Almost immediately there is a junction, with a path carrying straight

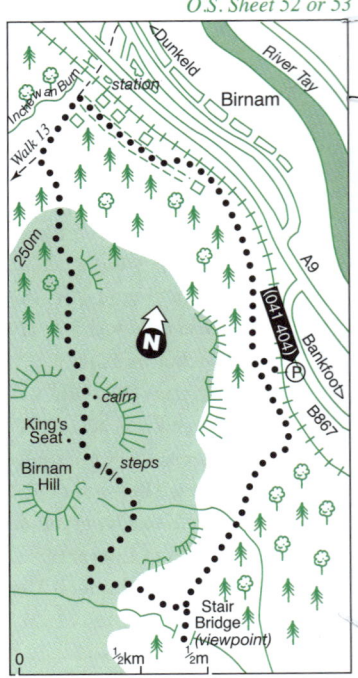

on to Birnam Station and the track turning right. Go right, through houses. When the houses end continue along the track, watching for a red arrow at the start of a rough path to the left. Follow this across the slope to join a track at a hairpin bend. Go left to return to the car park.

15 Loch Freuchie _____ B

A moderately long but technically easy walk around a small Highland loch; half on clear tracks and half on a quiet public road. Grazing cattle. Length: **8 miles/13km**; *Height Climbed:* **165ft/50m**.   *O.S. Sheet 52*

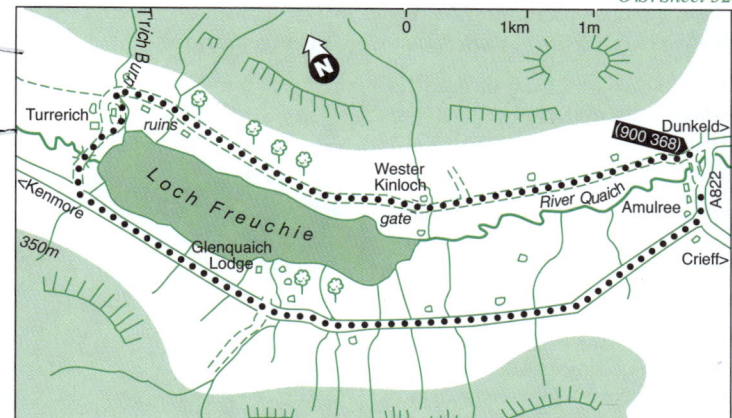

Amulree is a tiny village, high up in the hills between Dunkeld and Crieff. One of General Wade's military roads (from Crieff to Aberfeldy) passed through Amulree, and Bonnie Prince Charlie stayed at the inn on his retreat northwards in 1746. The village itself was built up around the junction of a number of cattle drove roads.

To reach Amulree, drive 9 miles west from Dunkeld on the A822 (Crieff) road.

Park in the village and walk north along the main road. Shortly before the road crosses the river the old road heads off to the left. Follow this across the old stone bridge. Just beyond, turn left onto a broad signposted track.

There is little difficulty with the route. The track starts above the river and then continues on the lightly wooded slope along the north-eastern side of Loch Freuchie. Beyond the north end of the loch the track crosses the Turrerich Burn and swings left; passing to the left of the farm, crossing the River Quaich beyond and then joining a narrow, quiet public road.

If you turn right along this road, you can follow it for 7 miles/11km (climbing to 1700ft/530m) to Kenmore, at the foot of Loch Tay – a fine walk with good views. For this route, however, turn left and follow the road back down Glen Quaich to the A822.

16 Harrietfield to Amulree — A

A moderately strenuous walk, through country little used by walkers. Good views ahead to Loch Freuchie on the final section. Length: **7 miles/11km** (one way); *Height Climbed:* **1300ft/400m**. *During normal shooting seasons, 12th August to 31st January each year, keep to the path and please pay attention to any signs on the route.*

O.S. Sheet 52

Harrietfield lies half-way up Glen Almond, just over the river from Glenalmond College. The walk starts 1/2 mile/0.8km to the west, at a hairpin bend in the road (Grid Ref 968 298). (NB: there is no parking at the start of the route and parking in Harrietfield is not easy either, so it is best to be dropped off at the start of the walk.)

Start walking up the access road for Logiealmond Estate, marked as the path to Amulree. After a short distance there is a split. Keep right and follow the metalled access road for a little over a mile/1.6km to reach a junction by the entrance to Logiealmond Lodge.

The lodge entrance is to your right and a clear track heads off to your left, but for this walk go ahead-left, up the western edge of the trees around the lodge grounds.

At the end of the trees you reach a gate. Go through this and follow the track uphill towards the spoil heaps of the old slate quarry, visible ahead. Pass through the quarry (please avoid climbing on the spoil heaps, which can be unstable).

The track climbs a little further beyond the quarry then descends into the next glen. At a junction keep right, heading up the glen. After half a mile/0.8km you reach another junction, level with a green shed down to your left. Keep right again (yellow arrow) and continue climbing to reach the pass at the head of the glen.

Beyond a gate near the highest point the track becomes rougher but remains clear, descending gradually to Girron before joining the public road 1/2 mile/0.8km short of Amulree.

17 **Little Glenshee to Strath Braan** ——————B

A moderate walk which gives the feeling of being amongst the hills, yet without involving great distance or ascent. Typical heathery hill country. Track or path all the way but possibly some wet going. Length: **4½ miles/7km** (one way); *Height Climbed:* **350ft/100m**.

O.S. Sheet 52

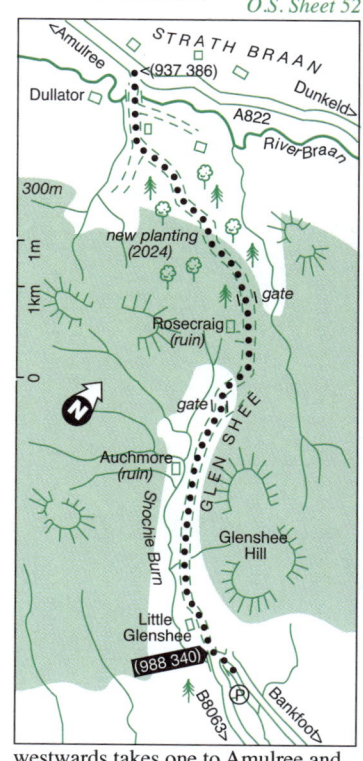

There are two roads to Little Glenshee Farm – one from the A9 north of Perth; the other from the B8063 along Glen Almond – which converge at a hairpin bend just short of the farm. There is a small car park by the ford over the burn. Cross a footbridge by the car park and follow the path/road to the hairpin bend.

A right of way sign at the start of the farm track points the way north to Strath Braan. The route passes the farm and continues up the glen on an obvious, rough track. There are no significant side-turnings or junctions for 2 miles/3km, until the track splits by a gate in a wall. Go through the gate and continue, climbing to the high point beyond the ruin at Rosecraig.

The descent on the north side is equally easy, following a clear track which passes through a number of gates on the way down, with occasional waymarkers/direction arrows, though these are more to help the southbound walker.

The north end of the route is marked by another right of way sign at the A822. Please note that it is difficult to park a car at this end of the route. If you need to, please ask permission at the nearby houses before doing so.

A walk of 2½ miles/4km westwards takes one to Amulree and the possibility either of returning to Glen Almond via Logiealmond (*see Walk 16*) or of continuing north-westwards by Loch Freuchie to Kenmore – *see Walk 15*).

18 Perth to Almondbank / 19 Perth to Luncarty_C/C

These two walks start from the centre of Perth and head north by the side of the River Tay: a chance to appreciate the might and charm of the river. At the junction with the River Almond the track splits: Walk 18 continuing by the leafy banks of the Almond to the cluster of settlements comprising Huntingtower, Almondbank and Pitcairngreen; Walk 19 following the Tay to Luncarty. **18)** *Length:* **5 miles/8km** *(one way); Height Climbed:* none. **19)** *Length:* **5 miles/8km** *(one way); Height Climbed:* none.

O.S. Sheet 53 or 58

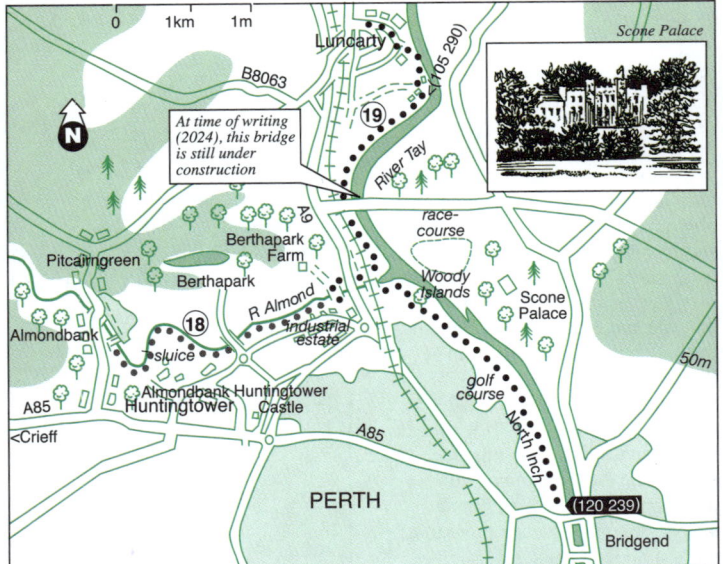

Start walking right in the heart of Perth, at Smeaton's fine old (1771) bridge linking the city to Bridgend. Below the city end of the bridge lies the little memorial park to the Cameronians and the 51st Highland Division, with an impressive list of their battle honours.

From here, the North Inch extends away upstream, as does the golf course and the city's flood prevention barriers. Walkers should be alert to the golfers' activities and give way as necessary. Beyond the golf course, the prospect to the north opens out, with fine views of the long curves of the river, while on the far side of the river are the wooded grounds of Scone Palace: a crenellated structure of red sandstone built in the early 19th century for the Earls of Mansfield. The route leads one past the Woody Islands and then begins to curve left, towards the confluence with the Almond.

Walk up the River Almond for a short distance, passing under the railway and the A9. Just before a third bridge crosses the way, the track splits.

Walk 18) To reach Almondbank, continue straight ahead, under the bridge. The route follows a tarred cycleway which starts running beside an industrial estate, then continues along the riverbank through pleasanter, leafy surroundings. There are no navigational difficulties, and the path eventually brings one to the sluice which controls the flow of water into the lade which once powered the mills of Perth. The route can be pursued a further 300-400m into the middle of Almondbank.

The name, incidentally, has nothing to do with almonds. It is derived from 'abhainn' – the Gaelic word for 'water' or 'stream'.

Almondbank/Huntingtower was once a significant centre for bleaching and dying, while the nearby Huntingtower Castle (open to the public), built in the 15th century, was the scene, in 1582, of the capture of the young James VI.

Walk 19) To reach Luncarty, go left, climbing to a cycle route junction then turning right, across the bridge. At the far end, just opposite the entrance to Berthapark Farm, turn right onto a woodland track and follow this back under the A9 and (ignoring the cycleway heading off to the left) the railway bridge beyond. Once past the railway the path swings left.

The path runs through woodland for a short way before rejoining the bank of the Tay and continuing upstream. The route crosses shortly into Redgorton Estate. The estate looks after its fishing clients well, and one passes along a pleasant gravel track with fishing bothies provided at the river's edge.

(**NB:** At time of writing (2024), a new road bridge is being built over the Tay. Please follow all instructions on the ground while this work is being undertaken, and any route changes once it is completed.)

The path leads on, without interruption or difficulty, to cottages at Grid Ref 105 290. The onward route lies on the landward side of the more northerly cottage and then back to the riverside, now on a narrow grass and earth path.

Approaching Luncarty, the path turns away from the river and follows the line of a small burn, down to your right, along the edge of a field. This leads to a flight of steps which climbs to join a metalled road.

To reach the centre of Luncarty, turn right along this road. This leads to the curved Lowfield Crescent. Turn left off this and follow roads through new housing to reach a shop, the B9099 and a bus stop.

20 Perth to Kinnoull Tower / 21 Kinnoull Hill / 22 Deuchny Wood ——————————— B/C/C

Three walks through the woodland behind a dramatic, rocky escarpment.
20) *A lineal climb from the centre of Perth to the tower on Kinnoull Hill. Magnificent views. Length:* **3 miles/5km** *(there and back); Height Climbed:* **720ft/220m**. **21)** *Three short waymarked walks through the woods on Kinnoull Hill. Length:* **¾-2 miles/1.2-3.3km**; *Height Climbed: undulating.* **22)** *A waymarked walk through the woods on Deuchny Hill, with possible extensions. Length: up to* **3½ miles/5.6km**; *Height Climbed:* **360ft/110m**. *NB: Cliff-top path. Please keep small children and animals under control at all times.*

O.S. Sheet 53 or 58

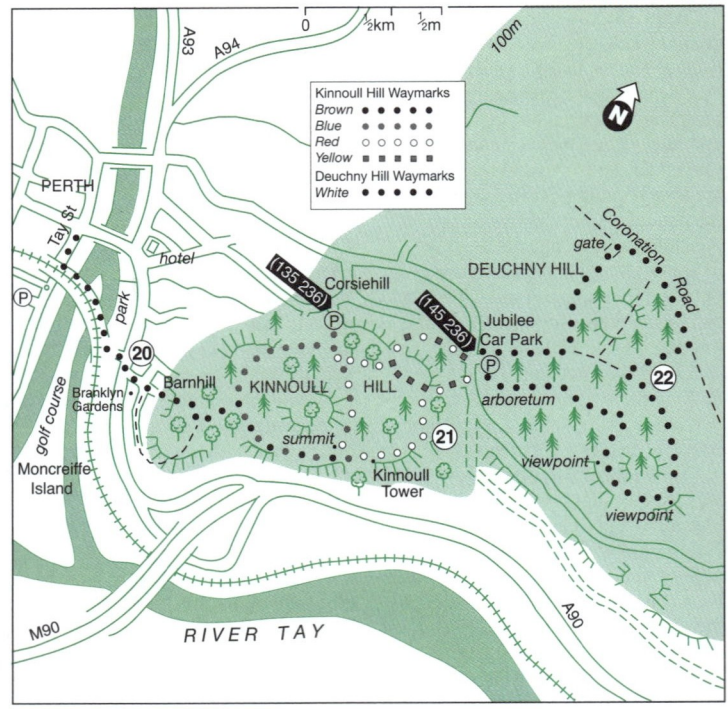

Kinnoull Hill, with its rocky escarpment above a steep wooded slope overlooking the Tay, dominates views of Perth from the south and east. The woods on and around the hill – and on the neighbouring Deuchny Hill – constitute Kinnoull Hill Woodland Park and contain some fine walks and spectacular views.

The hill can be reached on foot from Perth (*see* Walk 20). Alternatively, there are two car parks for the Park: Jubilee Car Park and the smaller Corsiehill Car Park (*see* map). To reach them by car, cross Perth Bridge (the more northerly of Perth's two road bridges) and keep straight ahead at the junction at its east end, climbing on a minor road. The car parks are signposted.

The most obvious landmark along these walks – and perhaps the best-known single image of Perth – is the cylindrical Kinnoull Tower, perched on the edge of the cliff above the River Tay. There are a variety of ways to reach the tower.

One option is to follow the driving instructions given above to reach the car parks. The shortest route to the Tower is from the Corsiehill Car Park. The circuit leading through the woods to the summit (1$^{1}/_{2}$ miles/2.5km) is marked by blue posts, and the tower is just to the east of the summit. Alternatively, you could park at Jubilee Car Park and follow the red circuit (2 miles/3.3km).

Walk 20 The most rewarding (if gruelling) walk to Kinnoull Tower is the steep climb from the centre of Perth. To do this, locate Tay Street, on the west side of the river, and walk to its southern end – where the railway bridge crosses the Tay. Climb the steps onto the bridge and cross the river, crossing Moncreiffe Island – with its allotments and golf course – on the way.

When the bridge reaches the far side avoid turning left, into the riverside park, and keep straight on until the metalled path turns left and climbs a lane with steps at its top end.

When you reach the road at the top of the lane cross straight over (carefully – it is busy) and turn right. After a short distance go ahead-left at the sign for Branklyn Garden.

The Garden is worth a visit in its own right, but for this walk turn left, at a junction just before the car park. Climb to a crossroads, where you have a choice. There are signs for Kinnoull Hill straight on and to the right. For this route, go straight on.

Climb to a further junction and go right (Kinnoull Hill). After a short distance there is a junction and a large map showing the routes in the Woodland Park. Turn left at this point on the Barnhill Trail, marked with brown posts.

Follow this uphill, through the trees, passing the junction with the alternative path and climbing to a signposted junction with the blue path. (Please note, there are numerous paths through the trees, not all waymarked. If you are uncertain at any junction, just keep going uphill until you join the blue route.)

Go right here (blue/brown) and follow the clear, cliff-top path to the summit. The prospect is magnificent, and the view down-river, with the ruined tower on the adjacent knoll, has appeared on many a postcard.

Those who know the major Perthshire hills will be able to pick out and name many familiar peaks from here, not to mention lower ranges such as the Ochils and the Lomonds of Fife. Directly across the Tay is Moncreiffe Hill (*see* Walk 26).

Continue along the cliff-tops (red) for a short way to reach the tower. This splendid folly was built in imitation of the defensive buildings seen flanking German rivers. It is not very old, having been built by the 9th Earl of Kinnoull in the 18th century.

Return by the same route or continue exploring the paths.

Walk 21) The best starting point for the waymarked walks is the Jubilee Car Park (*see* directions on previous page). There are three colour-coded circuits through the woods on Kinnoull Hill, two of which start from this car park. Cross the road from the car park to enter the woods, following a clear track. After a short distance there is a signposted fork. Keep left.

The shorter walk is marked by yellow posts; the longer by red. Both pass through pleasant, mixed woodland. The yellow route gives fine views, but does not approach the cliff top. The red route follows the cliffs for part of its length, passing Kinnoull Tower along the way, and joins with the blue route to make a longer walk.

Walk 22) There is one waymarked route through the woods on Deuchny Hill, starting from Jubilee Car Park. At the far end of the car park look for a clear path to the right of an interpretive panel (Deuchny Trail) marked by white posts.

The path runs through the Aitken Arboretum initially, before climbing out into the woodland. There is no difficulty following the route, with all junctions clearly marked.

The path makes an anti-clockwise circuit of the hill, passing a viewpoint looking over Kinoull Tower (Walk 20) and then a further viewpoint over the River Tay to the hills of Fife. The route includes a section on the Coronation Road – a bridleway following the old royal road between Falkland Palace and Scone.

There are two signposted short-cuts back to the Jubilee Car Park (*see* map), but if you ignore these you will end up walking around the north end of the hill before dropping back down to the car park.

Kinnoull Tower

23 **Bankfoot to Rumbling Bridge** ─────────── B

A pleasant, low hill crossing through farmland, moorland and woodland. Length: **8 miles/13km** (one way); *Height Climbed:* **600ft/180m** (south to north), **650ft/200m** (north to south).

O.S. Sheet 52 or 53

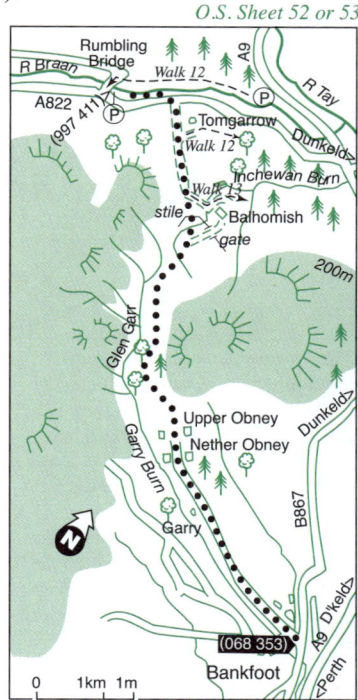

Bankfoot is a village just off the A9, 5 miles north of Perth. Park here (there are also bus services from Perth and Dunkeld) and walk west from the main street up Prieston Road. When you reach a junction, near the edge of the village, carry straight on, with the Garry Burn to your left.

The first section of the route follows a quiet public road, climbing 3 miles/5km through farmland to end at Upper Obney Farm. Pass through the gate and swing half-left through the buildings to reach a track beyond. Once clear of the farm the route crosses a stile and continues as a tractor track on the right-hand edge of a field. Walk straight ahead through the farmland until, at the end of the top field, you swing slightly to the left to reach a gate at a gap in a dyke.

This leads to the start of a clear, rough path, swinging first left then right into the narrow, wooded Glen Garr. Follow the path up to the watershed on the moorland above the glen and then down the other side.

The path crosses the upper waters of the Inchewan Burn. Shortly beyond this it splits. Turn onto the rougher, left-hand path (arrow) and drop down to cross the marshy burn, then climb beyond to a gate and stile with a fence to the left.

Cross the stile and continue on a grassy path which gradually converges with a track, visible down to the right. Follow this down to the junction with another track: keep straight on here to reach the public road, then follow the reverse of Walk 12 for a short distance to reach the car park at Rumbling Bridge.

24 Dunsinane Hill   B/C

A stiff hill-climb – short on distance, long on history – with the option of continuing to King's Seat, the highest point in the western Sidlaws. Excellent views. **Dunsinane only:** *Length:* **¾ mile/1.2km** (there and back); *Height Climbed:* **360ft/110m. King's Seat:** *Length:* **4½ miles/7km** (there and back); *Height Climbed:* **940ft/290m**.   O.S. Sheet 53

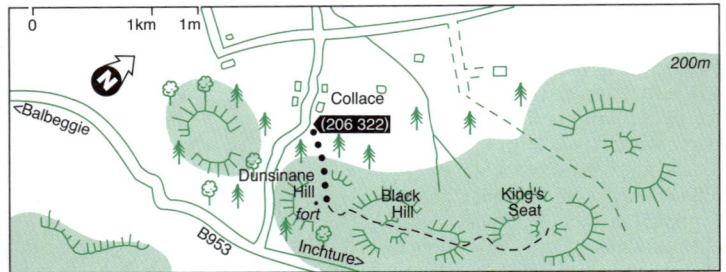

The starting point is just beyond the southern edge of the village of Collace, at a sharp bend in the road. There is an information board here and parking space for three or four cars (be careful not to block the field entrance).

Pass through the pedestrian gate and start climbing, having noted the advice regarding dogs (this is sheep country) and the possible presence of a bull in the field in the summer.

The way is perfectly clear – straight up the hill, until you can go no further! Approaching the summit, it is apparent that one is clambering over the concentric ramps and ditches which were constructed to add to the site's natural defensive qualities.

The pattern of defences is best seen from the next hill to the east, Black Hill, and visitors are strongly encouraged to go at least far enough up to be able to look down on Dunsinane, when the 'bird's eye view' reveals its military qualities dramatically. As there is 'no show without Punch', so there is no Dunsinane without Birnam Wood (Walk 14), and the sharp-eyed visitor, by careful study of the OS map, should be able to pick out the position of Birnam Wood, some 12 miles/20km away (Grid Ref 045 395). (*Macbeth*, Act IV Scene I and Act V, Scenes III and V).

For those wanting a longer walk, King's Seat lies 1½ miles/2.5km away to the north-east. It should be noted that this is rough walking with only vague sheep paths, and walkers should satisfy themselves that their presence will not impinge upon grouse-shooting or lambing. If in doubt, plan in advance and ask.

Return by the same route.

25 Errol & Port Allen_____C

This walk offers an insight into a different face of Perthshire from the familiar 'hill and heather' image: riverside reed-beds, rich farmland and views of the north Fife hills, all tucked away in a fold of the land which effectively cuts out the noise of the nearby Perth-Dundee road and railway. Length: **3 miles/5km**; *Height Climbed:* **160ft/50m**.

O.S. Sheet 53

To reach the little village of Errol, in the flat land of the Carse of Gowrie, drive east from Perth on the A90 for 5 miles and watch for a sign. There is usually room for roadside parking.

The main street in Errol is a long slope up from east to west; this walk starts down the little street leading south from Queen Victoria's Diamond Jubilee memorial beside the shops at the top end of the village (Gas Brae).

The village drops away on the south side and views open out down to the farmland which extends towards the River Tay. Once past the last houses, one can look down the estuary to the Tay bridges.

Beyond the edge of the village, the tarred road gives way to a clear footpath, flanked by a line of trees, which leads directly towards the river. After 1/2 mile/0.8km one reaches the edge of a wood flanking the estuary. At this point the track swings to the left – signposted as a path to Errol – and a cottage is visible directly ahead.

Leave the track and walk straight on, watching for a narrow path starting through the trees to your right. This is the next part of the walk, but it is worth continuing straight ahead for a short distance – to the right of the cottage – to gain some

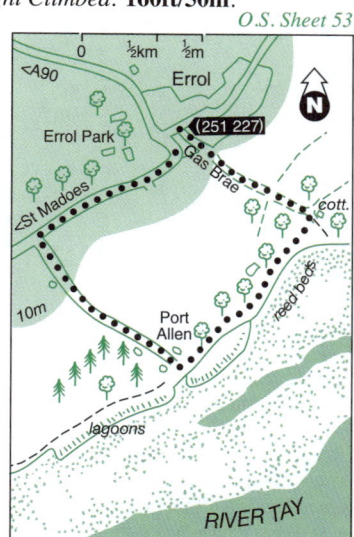

impression of the extensive reed-beds. The reeds were used in the past for thatching, and are still harvested.

Return to the junction and follow the path through the trees westwards. After 1/2 mile/0.8km this leads to a cluster of houses at Port Allen, where the harbour works are still evident.

From here, a narrow road leads away from the shore and up to the St Madoes-Errol road, along which a pavement leads all the way back to the starting point.

26 Moncreiffe Hill _____ B/C

*A network of three gentle forest walks providing good views of Kinnoull Hill and Perth, the Ochils, the North Fife hills and the lower reaches of the Rivers Earn and Tay. Lengths: **2-4½ miles/3-7.2km**; Height Climbed: up to **720ft/220m**.*

O.S. Sheet 58

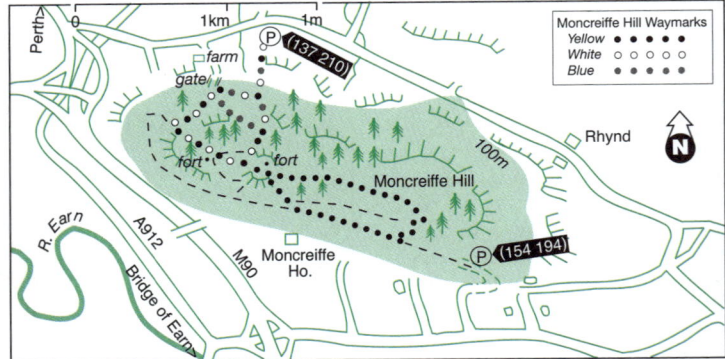

Moncreiffe Hill is a prominent wooded ridge just north of Bridge of Earn – when you drive north, the M90 cuts through its western end. The remains of two ancient hill forts can be seen on the hill, which is believed once to have been a site of some importance. The woodland on the hill is now administered by Woodland Trust Scotland, who have laid out three waymarked routes for walkers.

There are two car parks giving access to the hill. **The way to the southern car park** is signposted from the bridge at the north end of Bridge of Earn. The car park is a little over a mile along this minor road, up a track to the left. **To reach the northern car park**, drive south from the centre of Perth on the A912 and watch for the road heading left (east) for Rhynd and Moncreiffe Hill. The car park is a mile along this road, to the right.

The longest route (yellow waymarkers: *see map*) is a circuit of the hill, including a climb to the remains of Moredun Top Fort on the summit. The views are terrific: north to Perth and the distinctive cliffs and tower of Kinnoull Hill (Walks 20 & 21); east down to the Tay Estuary.

In addition, there are two shorter waymarked walks from the northern car park, blue (shortest) and white (*see map*), the latter of which also takes you past the summit fort. Information boards are available along the routes, and there are large-scale maps of the walks in both car parks.

27 **Dunbarney & Silver Walks** _____ **C**

Two short, flat, signposted walks which combine to form a half-circle around Bridge of Earn, taking in Dunbarney, Pitkeathly and Kintillo. Good views of Moncreiffe Hill and the northern flank of the Ochils. Length: **3¾ miles/6km**; *Height Climbed:* negligible.

O.S. Sheet 58

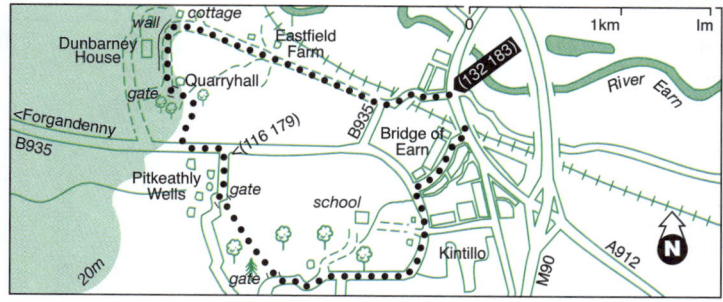

From the centre of Bridge of Earn, take the Forgandenny road (the B935). Beyond the edge of the village the road zig-zags over the railway; 100m further on, at the next bend, the road turns left and a clear access road goes straight on, signposted for Dunbarney Estate.

Follow the tarred road beyond, passing Eastfield Farm (to your right) and ignoring some private entrances to the left. The track eventually turns left at a cottage (becoming rougher), where it meets the high garden wall of Dunbarney House. Some attractive glimpses of the house and the gardens can be had over the next 100m. At the next right-angled bend, at Quarryhall, a sign points left, down a clear track along the side of the Quarryhall garden. At the end of the garden keep straight on along a path.

The remainder of this part of the route is along a narrow grassy track, between hedges and fields, with views ahead (southwards) to the Ochils. After 400m, the path reaches the B935 again, where a sign indicates the reverse route and also the way (100m along the road) to the start of the Silver Walk.

At a T-junction a minor road leads south to Pitkeathly Wells. Turn right. Some 300m south from the junction a sign for the walk points left, off the road. The path meanders between hedges and trees to a minor road running east-west, parallel to and south of the B935.

From here, the circuit can be completed by following the road, which skirts two sides of the grounds of Kilgraston School. Continue past the school entrance then turn right down Heughfield Road to return to Bridge of Earn.

28 Abernethy Glen — C

A light, waymarked stroll through mixed woodland and grazing land, with a possible extension up a low hill providing fine views of the Tay Estuary. Length: **1½-3 miles/2.5-5km**; Height Climbed: **300ft/90m** (**650ft/200m** if Castle Law is climbed).

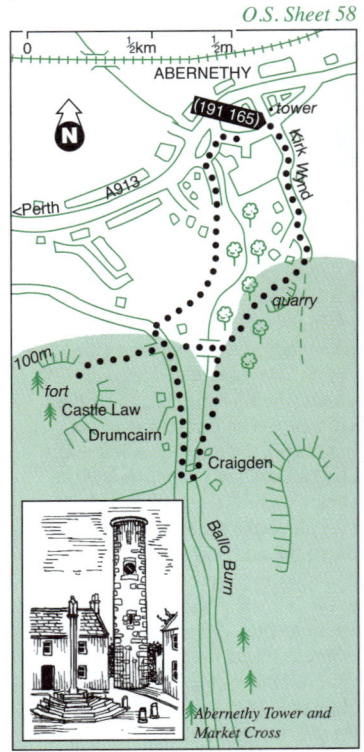

O.S. Sheet 58

Abernethy is a picturesque village 6 miles/9.5km south-east of Perth along the A912/A913. It is situated near the confluence of the Earn and the Tay, with the steep face of the Ochils at its back. It has a long history, the most obvious relic of which is the splendid Abernethy Round Tower: a 74ft high structure believed to date from the 11th century.

Start from the tower, walking south through the square then edging left to reach the start of Kirk Wynd. Follow this as it runs past house entrances before becoming a path. At a signposted junction keep right, walking across the face of the hill with a disused quarry to your left.

A little further on the path enters the wooded glen of the Ballo Burn and splits. For the shorter alternative route, cross the footbridge here (*see* map). To walk the full route, walk up the glen to join a quiet public road.

Turn right down this. Ignore the first signposted track to your left (Castle Law via Ayton Woods) and continue to the second (Castlelaw). If you wish to take on this short, brisk climb, the clear track will take you, zig-zagging, to the rubble walls of an Iron Age hill fort and to some splendid views.

Once back on the road, continue downhill for a short distance then turn right at a sign for a path to Abernethy. Follow this down to the western end of the village and turn right to return to the start.